MW01125277

Breaking the Addictive Cycle:

Deadly Obsessions or
Simple Pleasures?

David Powlison

New
Growth
Press
www.newgrowthpress.com

New Growth Press, Greensboro, NC 27404
Copyright © 2010 by David Powlison.
All rights reserved. Published 2010.

Typesetting: Robin Black, www.blackbirdcreative.biz

ISBN-10: 1-935273-19-1
ISBN-13: 978-1-935273-19-6

Library of Congress Cataloging-in-Publication Data

Powlison, David, 1949-
    Breaking the addictive cycle : deadly obsessions or simple pleasures? / David Powlison.
        p. cm.
    Includes bibliographical references and index.
    ISBN-13: 978-1-935273-19-6
    ISBN-10: 1-935273-19-1
1. Compulsive behavior. I. Title.
RC533.P69 2010
    616.85′84—dc22
    2010002963

Printed in China

25 24 23 22 21 20 19 18   11 12 13 14 15

Stacie loves to shop. She often plans her whole day around going to her favorite stores. Getting something new always makes her happy…for a while. But soon she notices something else she really "needs." She spends a lot of time thinking about (and plotting how to make) her next purchase. Lately, she hasn't told her husband when she goes shopping because "he would just get upset." Stacie knows she is spending too much money and time buying stuff, but she doesn't know how to stop.

Kyle likes playing video games. He especially gets absorbed in the complicated, role-playing games—playing them for hours, days, weeks. He spends most of his free time on the computer. His wife complains that he spends far more time playing video games than he does with her and the children or on household responsibilities. When she goes to bed, he goes on the computer. It's just easier if she doesn't know exactly how long he is playing. He knows he is slacking off at work because he's tired from being up all night. Every morning he thinks, *I won't get on the computer tonight after work*, but somehow he always does.

Jamie enjoys eating. In fact, she enjoys food so much that she plans her route to work so she can stop at her favorite donut shop. At work, she maintains a private stash of snacks in her desk "just in case I need a little pick-me-up." All morning she thinks about what she will order for lunch, and then it's on to planning a big dinner. Sometimes she gets up late at night and finishes all the leftovers from dinner. Her blood sugar and cholesterol numbers are too high. Her weight is climbing. Jamie knows she should cut back on food, but whenever she tries to diet, she thinks about food even more.[1]

It's easy to see that Stacie, Kyle, and Jamie are looking for pleasure, but the harder they try to find it, the less pleasure they feel. Instead, they've become obsessed with getting more and more of what once gave them enjoyment. Their pleasures deliver less and less, and come at a greater cost to family, pocketbook, and health. The things they pursue are not the hardcore "addictions"—things that are illegal, immoral, and obviously self-destructive. They are not the textbook "obsessive-compulsive disorders." But any pleasure running amok becomes an obsession and a compulsion. They clearly illustrate the addictive cycle. Understanding "little" addictions helps us to understand the big addictions. The solution turns out to be exactly the same! And it begins with understanding God's good gift of pleasure.

Simple Pleasures Are Good

It would be easy to think that the solution to Stacie, Kyle, and Jamie's problems (and yours) is to reject all pleasure and enjoyment. But just becoming more disciplined ignores how God made us. God made us to feel. Something is missing if we don't ask questions about what is beautiful, about joy and sorrow, pleasure and pain, adoration and disgust. It can be hard for us to understand that pure pleasure was created "very good." And it is hard for us to understand how pleasure is being recreated by Jesus as "very, very good."

People often say, "I don't want to become a Christian because I'll have to give up the ten things I most love doing and do the ten things I most hate doing." These people don't realize that the things on their list are false. They don't understand exactly how pleasure is wired into human experience.

What gives *you* pure and simple pleasure? What truly refreshes you? What helps you to lay your cares down and get a fresh perspective on life? What enables you to step back into the business and hardship of life with a new joy?

My own list includes lighting up when I see an old friend. I'm so glad to see someone I love. A particular meal can evoke warm memories that take me back to childhood joys. And for simple pleasure, there is nothing finer than shooting hoops. One time I hit forty-seven straight free throws!

In a novel by Patrick O'Brian, a man considers whether to buy an Amati violin. He loves music, but the violin is costly. His friend says to him, "Certainly you must have your fiddle. Any innocent pleasure is a real good. There are not so many of them."[2] In other words, "This is something truly good. Do it. Spend the money."

Sex should be on the list of pure pleasures. Because of sin, sex gets a bad name. But in the Bible, sex within marriage is an unstained, erotic joy. God made it, so it is very good. It's the same with enjoying a good meal. In our society food takes on ugly and false meanings: Salvation? Poison? Fat calories? Escape? But it does not need to mean these things. We can say, "Thank you, God, for daily bread."

The Psalms revel in creation. We marvel at the unparalleled beauty of a sunrise and sunset, and even more at a Master Artist so creative that he will erase his art every day to begin again the next.

So many simple, unstained pleasures: Collecting stones on a lakeshore. Watching autumn leaves drop. Innocent pleasures are a means to step away from what is hard, wearisome, or difficult in our lives into something restful and beautiful. They are not an escape from life's troubles, they are meant to refresh and strengthen us.

What makes such pleasures innocent? It is the fact that there is a *greater* pleasure. That greatest pleasure is the Maker of all the innocent ones. Is devotion to God one of your pleasures? Perhaps pure pleasure comes to you in worship, through certain hymns or the celebration of the Lord's Supper. Whenever I read the Gospel of Luke, I rejoice in its picture of the tenderness of Jesus with the broken of the earth. The lesser innocent pleasures come because the greatest pleasure, God himself, is in his rightful place.

Innocent pleasures don't pretend to save you or protect you. They don't promise you meaning and identity in life. They don't take life's fragility, pain, frustration, disappointment, and uncertainty and wash them away. They are not the giver of every good and perfect gift; they are just gifts you enjoy. They are innocent because they don't pretend to be anything more.

Trapped in an Addictive Cycle

What makes a pleasure go bad? How did clothing, recreation, and tasty food go bad for Stacie, Kyle, and Jamie? Think about this in your own life. Which entertainments contain a quality of obsession, residual guilt, or anxiety? Which recreations bring disappointment?

Which amusements tend to hijack you, promising to make you feel good, but then failing? Perhaps like Stacie you are obsessed with shopping, or like Kyle you can't seem to stop playing video games, or you might struggle like Jamie with food. Or perhaps you are addicted to the heavy-hitters: alcohol, drugs, sex. In our world there are so many choices. There are as many different obsessions as there are different types of people.

What are the guilty pleasures in your life? The obvious ones would be immorality, anger, self-righteousness, alcohol and drug abuse, and the like. But what about the things that are, in and of themselves, okay? They are good—or at least not bad. Yet they can capture your heart and become too important in your life. What is on your list of potentially innocent pleasures that go bad?

What about this list? Browsing a catalog. Checking email many times a day. Talking on the phone. How about reading novels—even good ones? It could be exercise, games or puzzles, talk radio, shopping or snacks between meals. There is nothing wrong with these activities in themselves. So how can you tell when a pleasure

crosses the line from innocent to guilty? Here are five
warning signs:

1. *The pleasure is plain wrong.* The activity is sinful
in and of itself. This includes drunkenness, illegal drug
use, lust, outbursts of anger, and gossip. These are the
easy ones to spot.

2. *The pleasure captivates and captures you.* The
activity is not sinful, but you become preoccupied with
it. You obsess and fantasize about it. You can't wait to
do it or have it. I remember one time driving to a con-
ference, and I suddenly realized that I'd been fantasiz-
ing about the Coke I would drink on the way home. I
thought, *I seriously need to get a life!* There is nothing
wrong with what I wanted to do, but why was my mind
parked there? It was a minor stained pleasure. It took up
too much mental space. It became too important.

Soon those pleasures don't just take mental space;
they require action. You become compulsive about it.
Every time you are bored and lonely, you flip on the
TV. Every time you feel hurt or stressed out, you eat.
It owns you. It masters you. Stacie's shopping falls into

this category. It's not wrong to buy clothes for yourself or your family, but Stacie was organizing her whole life around her desire to buy things.

Every human being is obsessive-compulsive. OCD is not so much a diagnosis as a description of humanity. Obsession means that something is too much on our minds. Compulsion means that something is too much in our actions. It leads to a stain. Paul says, "All things are lawful for me, but not all things are profitable….I will not be mastered by anything" (1 Corinthians 6:12, NASB).

3. *The pleasure is hidden.* This is a real tip-off. It may be an innocent thing to do, but you hide it. Why? When you create a secret garden of any sort in your life, mutant things always grow. They might start out as beautiful roses but they turn ugly when they grow in secret. Everything should be open to inspection, because in fact they are always seen by someone. There are no secrets before the Lord. Notice how Stacie, Kyle, and Jamie are trying to hide what they are doing.

4. *The pleasure steals you away from the good.* A guilty pleasure steals you away from the good things you ought

to be doing. You should call your sister, but you read magazines for two hours. You should pay your bills, but you check e-mail. The bills start to clutter up tomorrow's schedule, and eventually this affects relationships. You're distracted and edgy, and you fail to love. It affects your job and your family.

5. *The pleasure doesn't deliver.* Stained pleasures are often subtle. We often do them because they seem to promise some sort of joy, satisfaction, refuge, or meaning. But stained pleasures never deliver. They leave you empty, anxious, guilty, more obsessed, and vaguely unhappy. You have to pull these guilty pleasures into the daylight to see them for what they are.

Using Pleasure to Escape Trouble

Stained and guilty pleasures often arise as a restless escape from troubles. Something in life is hard and we want a break. They promise good things but never deliver them. Instead, they leave you with queasy feelings.

What difficulties tempt you towards the guilty pleasures? Here are three broad categories:

- When you are bored and lonely, with nothing to do, you _____.
- When you are stressed, frustrated, and worn out, you _____.
- When you are hurt, betrayed, and treated unfairly (perhaps grieving a loss, perhaps aggrieved at unfair treatment), you _____

_____.

These kinds of situations tend to lead us away from innocent pleasures to the stained and guilty ones. We grab for anything that will protect, soothe, comfort, or save us. This raises a crucial issue in how you think about pleasure: *How do you face pain?* What do you do with hardships? As Stacie, Kyle, and Jamie learn to answer this question, they will be well on their way to redeeming pleasure and escaping the hold that guilty pleasures have on them.

Go to God with Your Pain

Scripture shows us that God runs his universe in ways that are counterintuitive. There is a surprising door to the greatest pleasure. It remakes the lesser, innocent pleasures, placing them in their proper place. That counterintuitive door is to face your suffering, to take hold of it instead of seeking to escape it. To stop what you are doing and honestly say to God, "I feel all alone right now. I'm tired. I'm bored. I'm hurt. I'm worried and stressed. But I know you are with me. I know you are my true refuge. Help me!" This is the counterintuitive door into joy.

Worship in the Bible expresses two things to God: our pain and our pleasure. For example, one aspect of the Old Testament sacrificial system is about guilt, need, suffering, and hardship. We need cleansing and deliverance. The other kinds of sacrifice express gratitude. We have been blessed, we have a harvest, we are feasting, and we enjoy peace. We bring to God both our pain and our pleasure.

Some psalms suffer honestly: "O God, I am in anguish. Deliver me from my sufferings and my sins." Other psalms delight honestly: "O my God, you are good. I thank you, worship you, and adore you." We speak both of pain and pleasure. Somehow, in the way God runs his universe, our willingness to enter into the experience of pain, disappointment, loneliness, hurt, and stress—being willing to face it and not bolt for some lesser pleasure—winds up being the door to the greatest pleasure of all. And with the best come the other true pleasures, felt deeply.

In 1 Peter 1, suffering is the context in which you experience "joy inexpressible and full of glory" (v. 8, NASB). In James 1, trial is the context of purpose, endurance, meaning, and joy. In Romans 5, we are told that "we rejoice in our suffering" (v. 3). In the midst of sorrows, anguish, misery, and pain we come to know that "the love of God has been poured out within our hearts through the Holy Spirit who was given to us" (v. 5, NASB). Walking into suffering with eyes wide open, and not running after escapist pleasures, opens the door to knowing the love of God.

In her hymn, "Be Still, My Soul," Katharina von Schlegel expressed great sorrow, yet a spring of life and joy wells up in the pain.

> Be still, my soul: the Lord is on thy side;
> bear patiently the cross of grief or pain;
> leave to thy God to order and provide;

in every change, he faithful will remain.

Be still, my soul; thy best, thy heav'nly Friend

through thorny ways leads to a joyful end.

Katharina von Schlegel understood that suffering tests whether our pleasure and hope are firmly attached to the one greatest pleasure, with the innocent pleasures following behind. In the *Book of Common Prayer*, the General Thanksgiving says, "We bless thee for our creation, preservation, and all the blessings of this life." We might paraphrase this, "We thank you for the innocent pleasures and the good things." But then this wise prayer goes on, "But above all [we thank thee] for thine inestimable love in the redemption of the world by our Lord Jesus Christ; for the means of grace, and for the hope of glory."[3] In the hands of a loving God, sorrow and suffering become doorways into the greatest and most indestructible joys.

The Joy Lever

Watch an elderly woman get exquisite pleasure from a sunbeam on the kitchen floor, or a well-brewed cup of tea. Her grandchild brings even greater joy. It takes less and less innocent pleasure to push the lever of joy. It's one of those secrets of the Christian life. Far from the belief that Christians have to give up everything they enjoy to do dreary things, the truth is that your pleasure mechanism is rearranged. You are freed to feel all sorts of exquisite joys you never imagined. It takes less and less effort.

In the stained pleasure cycle, the addictive cycle, it takes more and more to push the lever of joy. Stained pleasures have this corroding effect: They always up the ante. You watch more movies and listen to more music. You exercise harder and longer. You think, *This video game isn't graphic enough. That vacation isn't exotic enough. This pornography isn't explicit enough. This amount of alcohol isn't enough.* The pleasures dull and sometimes completely disappear. You get no satisfaction from eating, yet you shovel food into your mouth anyway. The drunk becomes somber and unhappy. The high from marijuana brings paranoid terror. The thrill of these guilty pleasures is gone.

Practical Strategies for Change

What pushes the lever of joy for you? Is it becoming harder and harder, or easier and easier? Are your pleasures innocent or stained? Let me suggest four action plans that will move you in the right direction. The first aims to cultivate innocent pleasures. The second aims to remove the stains that pervert pleasure. The third gives you direction on how to grow in the pleasure of knowing God. The fourth will encourage you to grow in the pleasure of knowing others.

Action Plan #1: Stop...and Really Enjoy Yourself

If you are the sort of person who dutifully presses on through life, take a break from your busyness. Step off the treadmill of duties at work, home, and church.

If you are the sort of person who rushes into recreation, take a break from your exercise, TV, hobbies, movies, video games, snacking, phone calls, and whatever.

Whether you live to work or live to play, stop to think about something very important:

- In your experience, what has proved *truly restful?*
- What has left you feeling *nourished* afterwards?

Think about this yourself, then talk it over with people close to you. Stick to the small, everyday things that don't take lots of time, effort, and money. What are the things you linger to appreciate, that give you a good, hearty laugh, leave you encouraged, or help you sleep? What tasks lead you to savor the achievement and give thanks to God? These innocent pleasures may involve your children, nature, exercise, creativity, music, or worship. Do you build joys such as these?

Second, what pleasures leave no residue, no guilt, exhaustion, or unrest? This can be a very revealing question. Do the things you do instinctively leave you refreshed or more restless? Compare the things you turn to for "a break" with the things that actually bring delight. God *made* us for rest and pleasure, and he wired us so that stained pleasures will leave a stain, while the innocent pleasures bring pure pleasure.

Third, what is the invigorating opposite of your workaday life? If you're a landscaper, sit down and read a good book. If you're a scholar, go and work in the garden. If you're a stay-at-home mom, arrange for someone to care for the kids. If you put in long hours at the office, take care of the kids. You get the idea. Honest work and honest rest are complementary goods. The Bible's view of rest ("sabbath") is not legalistic; it's restful and refreshing. And since God tailor-makes everyone different, what's deeply pleasurable will vary from one person to the next.

Action Plan #2: Take a Fast from Your Obsession

What forms of pleasure do you pursue impulsively or compulsively? Perhaps you are struggling with behaviors that were never innocent pleasures. You are obsessed with doing things that are just plain wrong—things such as sexual immorality, alcohol, or drug abuse. The pleasure you feel was never innocent and good—it was always stained, always guilty. If that is true for you, then your fast needs to be permanent. You probably already know that giving up your obsession is easier to talk about than to do. But the path of change for you in this area is the same path that everyone who wants to change must take. Don't despair. Keep reading. Use the action steps below to get a handle on how to think, pray, and involve others in your struggle to give up your obsession. And please don't stop with reading this minibook. Ed Welch has written an excellent, biblical, guide to help you turn from your addiction, *Crossroads: A Step-by-Step Guide Away from Addiction.*[4]

Or maybe you are more like Stacie, Kyle, and Jamie— you are obsessed with a once innocent pleasure. You look forward *too much* to that cup of coffee, that donut, that book. Do you jump into it *too automatically?* Whatever it is that has captured your attention, your thought life, and your desires—take a one-week break from it.

Perhaps that doesn't sound like much; perhaps it sounds impossible! Either way, view it as a holy experiment. An intentional fast from your recreation habits works against your obsessive pleasure-seeking and teaches you fascinating things about yourself and your God.

What happens when you fast?

1. *You struggle.* You try not to watch TV all evening. You try not to stop at your favorite store. You try to ignore the last brownie in the pan. But it's not easy! The first time you don't give in to your obsession, you think, *I want to do it; I need to do it. I can't give this up.* You find that your obsession has a hold on you. Such things don't let up their grip just because you planned a week-long break. You discover the power of the desire when you try to give it up. This simple thing has power over you!

2. *You rationalize.* You will think, *If I don't do it, I'll be bored. What will I do without it?* Perhaps you get a bit edgy or irritable. Perhaps you feel bored or adrift. Perhaps you find yourself daydreaming about the pleasures you are missing or the trouble that might happen if

you don't do this. Perhaps you start to rationalize: "This fast is stupid!" and "What's the big deal ?" and "It's not wrong to eat, so I don't care." Perhaps you think you would rather start this project tomorrow instead. But here's where the battle shows its face. Here it becomes clear that you are tangled up in something that has enslaved you.

3. *You see your need for Jesus.* When you really experience the power of your obsession, you see that you need outside help to give it up. You see how much you need Jesus' mercy and help. Whether you are fasting from something small like drinking a Coke or something large like drug abuse, you see that you need your Savior to deliver you. You realize how strong your lusts are. You realize that you have used your obsession to medicate yourself. So you call out to Jesus for help. This is your time of need. He promises to help you when you cry to him for mercy and help (Hebrews 4:14–16). As you recognize the battle you are in and beg Jesus for help, you will find that he does help. He is an ever-present help to sinners. Your faith will awaken. You will no longer be aimlessly drifting through

life, trying to escape hardship and suffering. You will walk with Jesus, your Savior and Helper.

4. *You discover other people.* Now that your struggle is out in the open in your own life, you can involve other people. Ask your friends and family to pray for you, to ask you how you are doing, and to encourage you. Now you can talk with them about what's really going on in your life—things you had kept secret, even from yourself. And, as you make even small headway, you will discover that faith always works through love. You think, *I don't have to go to the fridge to eat. I can call my friend Suzie who is going through a hard time. I can read a story to my child. I can take a walk with my husband.* Your life becomes richer in real relationships. You discover the joy of being with people.

5. *Your joy increases.* It's amazing how much joy you can have in the smallest of things. When you don't spend all your time playing video games, you can take the time to watch the leaves falling from the maple tree. You go outside and look for the first star and notice the full moon. When you aren't anesthetizing yourself, it

takes less and less to push the lever of joy in your life. There's a new spring in your step, and more solid joy in your heart.

Action Plan #3: Grow Your Relationship with God

What will give you the most pleasure in life? What pleasure will not dim through all the changes of your life? The pleasure of knowing God and being known by him. You step into that pleasure by coming to Jesus for mercy and grace. You grow in your relationship with him by making that call for mercy a daily, life-long habit. Your inability to deal with your obsessions is God's mercy to you, because it forces you to go to God for the help you need. As you go to God, use his Word to guide your relationship.

Psalm 23 has been my prayer for many years. Praying through it is one way to experience the pleasure of a growing relationship with God. Start by reading it out loud.

> The LORD is my shepherd, I shall not be in want.
> > He makes me lie down in green pastures,

he leads me beside quiet waters,

    he restores my soul.

He guides me in paths of righteousness

    for his name's sake.

Even though I walk

    through the valley of the shadow of death,

I will fear no evil,

    for you are with me;

your rod and your staff,

    they comfort me.

You prepare a table before me

    in the presence of my enemies.

You anoint my head with oil;

    my cup overflows.

Surely goodness and love will follow me

    all the days of my life,

and I will dwell in the house of the Lord

    forever.

Notice how the psalmist takes hold of suffering. He looks the shadow of death right in the eye: "I will fear no evil." He knows the Lord is with him. Notice how he switches from talking about God in the third person ("he") to the second person ("you") in an amazing expression of intimacy with God. The last two lines say that goodness and lovingkindness are literally chasing him! "I am being pursued by your goodness and mercy all my life, and then I will live with you forever." This is the supreme pleasure.

Now take a moment to rewrite this psalm to reflect your life. How has Jesus been your Good Shepherd? What places of beauty, peace, and safety has he led you to? Thank him for the ways he has guided you. What hard times has he walked with you through? Can you say with faith that "goodness and love will follow me all the days of my life"? When these things are hard for you to pray, ask Jesus to teach you about himself. Go to John 10 and read about Jesus, the Good Shepherd. Ask him to give you the joy of hearing him call you by name, of knowing that he is walking with you. These are prayers that God delights to answer. He promises that when you seek him, you will find him (Jeremiah 29:13). When you find God, you find the greatest pleasure there is.

Action Plan #4: Grow Your Relationship with People

One step behind the supreme pleasure of loving God is the pleasure of true friendship—loving others. We sometimes get confused about the fact that there are people we deeply enjoy. Perhaps you've heard that *agape* love is an act of the will, contrary to how you feel. We know that the Bible tells us that we shouldn't just hang out with our friends. We should reach out to people who are different from us, to the stranger, and even to our enemies. We might start to think that the paradigm for relationships is, *To really love people, I should associate with people I don't like; with people who are tough to get along with, manipulative, neurotic, high maintenance, awkward, and aggressive—people who require a lot of effort!* But something is wrong with that view. You say, "I really like these other people! They are my friends, people I respect. They love me and help me. Does that mean I *shouldn't* pursue people if we care about each other?" That can't be it!

The Bible holds these two pictures of relationship in tension. The leading theme, the richer theme, involves the people you truly enjoy—your beloved brother, sister, wife, the child you hold in your arms, and dear friends. In heaven you will see face-to-face the One you love, the supreme Person. But heaven is also a place full of other relationships you enjoy. These people love you without pretense, competition, or manipulation.

But side by side with that call to joyous intimacy is a call to get out of your comfort zone. The harder call of the Bible is to love enemies, strangers, people who are different from you, and those who are needy, sinful, and broken.

This call comes for two reasons. First, it tests whether you are turning the innocent pleasures of intimacy into a stained pleasure. Are you and the people you enjoy turning into a clique? Second, the call tests whether we are willing to widen the circle of intimacy so that enemies become friends, strangers become like family, and someone you don't know becomes like a dear sister. The goal is always the simple, joyous relationship with others——the mutual affection and give-and-take. God calls you to widen the circle of your friendships, and to avoid making a god out of those who bring you the greatest pleasure. Doing these two things will fill your life with the pleasure of growing relationships with others.

The Redemption of Pleasure

Perhaps as you read this minibook you are seeing for the first time how little true pleasure is in your life and how much of your life is captured by obsessions. Don't despair. God freely gives himself. The Father's love, the Son's self-sacrifice, the Spirit's intimate power are freely offered gifts. God is committed to helping you turn away from obsession and towards the true pleasure of loving God and others.

The restoration of true pleasure in your life is one of the prime works of the Holy Spirit. When you are caught in the bipolar swing between anxious responsibilities and escapist feel-good obsessions, he will shake you loose. He will patiently teach you to live out God's will and grow in your love for God and people. He will free you from obsessively chasing the lesser pleasures—those things that never deliver and always disappoint. His help is yours for the asking. Turn to God in faith. Ask for forgiveness for Jesus' sake for all the ways you turn from him. Ask the Spirit to come into your heart and change you. God will answer this prayer. Perhaps you won't see dramatic change in the next five minutes or five days, but you will see change in the long run. Keep going to God and you will notice—whether in minutes, days, months, or years—that you have more of the true pleasure that comes from knowing and trusting God.

Endnotes

1 All names are fictitious and personal details have been changed.
2 Patrick O'Brian, *Post Captain* (New York: W. W. Norton, 1972), 60.
3 *Book of Common Prayer* (New York: Oxford University Press, 1935), 19.
4 Edward T. Welch, *Crossroads: A Step-by-Step Guide Away from Addiction* (Greensboro, NC: New Growth Press, 2008).

Simple, Quick, Biblical
Advice on Complicated Counseling Issues
for Pastors, Counselors, and Individuals

MINIBOOK
CATEGORIES

- Personal Change
- Marriage & Parenting
- Medical & Psychiatric Issues

- Women's Issues
- Singles
- Military

USE YOURSELF | GIVE TO A FRIEND | DISPLAY IN YOUR CHURCH OR MINISTRY

New Growth Press

Go to **www.newgrowthpress.com** or call **336.378.7775** to purchase individual minibooks or the entire collection. Durable acrylic display stands are also available to house the minibook collection.